The not-for-profit **Outriders Poetry Project** was founded in 1968 by Doug Eichhorn, Dan Murray and Max Wickert. With partial support from Poets & Writers and the New York State Council of the Arts, we have sponsored numerous readings, and have published work by writers living in, or significantly associated with, the Buffalo-Niagara region. Since 2010, we have been operating chiefly as a small press. Submissions in competition for new books are considered each year between January 1 and April 15.

For further details, check our website
http://www.outriderspoetryproject.com/

or write to:

Outriders Poetry Project
314 Highland Avenue
Buffalo, New York 14222
Email: *outriderspoetry@me.com*

herein.

Additionally, the information in the following pages is intended only for informational purposes and should thus be thought of as universal. As befitting its nature, it is presented without assurance regarding its prolonged validity or interim quality. Trademarks that are mentioned are done without written consent and can in no way be considered an endorsement from the trademark holder.

VIP Subscriber List

Dear Reader, If you would like to receive latest tips and tricks on internet marketing, exclusive strategies, upcoming books & promotions, and more, do subscribe to my mailing list in the link below! I will be giving away a free book that you can download right away as well after you subscribe to show my appreciation!

Here's the link: http://bit.do/jonathanswalker

TABLE
OF
CONTENTS

Introduction

Congratulations on purchasing your personal copy of *Affiliate Marketing: Build Your Own Successful Affiliate Marketing Business from Zero to 6 Figures.* Thank you for doing so.

The following chapters will discuss everything that you need to know in order to grow an affiliate marketing business for yourself. Everyone wishes that they could start a passive income business on the internet, and this book is going to show you how to do exactly that. By the end of this book, you'll know the specific steps to take in order to become an affiliate marketing guru. While it takes some time and dedication to get started, once you learn the basics you'll be able to develop a reputable and sound online business for yourself and make fewer mistakes along the way.

You will discover why affiliate marketing is considered by many people to be a fabulous way to earn passive income on the internet, along with all of the tools that you'll need to get started. This book will also go into the different types of affiliate marketing, and even how to begin advertising with Amazon. Amazon is arguably the largest online marketplace on the internet right now and is also one of the most popular sources for affiliate marketers to flock. If you can join the ranks of these people who are already working with Amazon, it's safe to say that you'll have "made it" in the affiliate marketing world.

There are plenty of books on affiliate marketing out there, thanks again for choosing this book! Every effort was made to ensure it is full of as much useful information as possible. Please enjoy!

Congratulations on purchasing your personal copy of *Affiliate Marketing: Build Your Own Successful Affiliate Marketing Business from Zero to 6 Figures*. Enjoy the rest of this book!

Chapter 1: Affiliate Marketing, Website Creation, and Keyword Research

Affiliate marketing on the internet can be best defined as when you, the website developer, creates a website that promotes other people's products. Whenever someone else's product sells due to traffic that has manifested on your website, you get paid a commission. One of the greatest advantages that affiliate marketing can provide an individual is that you do not need to develop an entirely new product on your own in order to see a profit. By focusing on website development, rather than product development, you're able to avoid high shipping and manufacturing costs. Two key aspects of affiliate marketing involve creating a website and conducting keyword research.

Creating a Website

You're not going to be able to become an affiliate

marketer without a website. This may sound daunting, but there are plenty of programs out there that can help you achieve this goal, including Wix, SquareSpace, and WordPress. WordPress is probably the best tool to use because it will rank better in the eyes of Google than will the other two options. The average cost of starting a website including the following:

Domain Name	$10 Per Year
Web Hosting	$10 Per Month
SEO Help	$10 Per Month
Total	$250 Annually

When you think about startup costs that are associated with other types of businesses, $250 is nothing! You can opt to skip the cost of SEO assistance, but you'll see in a minute why you definitely don't want to do that.

SEO, Keyword Research, and Niche Topics

An essential aspect of good affiliate marketing involves setting up your website to revolve around a niche topic that is going to attract a specific client base. The competition on the internet is fierce, which is why this research step is essential prior to setting up your website. To achieve this, you are going to need to becoming acquainted with SEO, or Search Engine Optimization. The first websites that come up when you type something into Google are ones that are great at meeting SEO standards. The administrators for these sites are keeping a close eye on what people like you and me are typing into Google in regards to the product that they're trying to sell. They are then making sure that the content on their website is meeting the needs of the keyword traffic that is coming through Google.

This is why SEO research is so important, and why you should opt to pay for help with SEO when you have this option. Some of the best SEO websites including the following:

1. Moz.com
2. Searchengineland.com
3. SEObook.com

When you go onto these websites, you're able to type in a keyword and find the amount of traffic that

Google is seeing for this particular word or phrase. Specifically for your website, you should be looking for a keyword that is related to a broad topic that has a high volume of searches, but a low amount of competition. For example, starting a website that advertises all yoga gear is not good enough; you're going to be competing with companies like Lululemon and Athleta. A niche site would instead be one that focuses only on new products in yoga props, for example. When you're researching for your website, make sure that your keyword is truly niche in nature. Try to be as detailed as possible.

Chapter 2: Essential Affiliate Marketing Tips

Once you have decided on your niche topic and have done extensive keyword research, your work is far from over. The next step is to develop your website. Affiliate marketers typically will use product reviews in order to see a profit. The basic premise here is to review products that people are searching frequently because these types of consumers want to be assured that they're buying a reliable product prior to purchase. Some of the basic types of posts that affiliate marketers will put on their sites include the following:

1. **Direct Posts:** These are product reviews. These reviews will include features about the product in question, and most importantly will have a link to purchase the product somewhere in the post.

2. **List Posts:** List posts are becoming more popular these days because they can be read quickly and can be easily shared on other sites such as Facebook or Twitter. Some great list posts include "How-to" posts or "10 Best" list posts.

3. **Indirect Posts:** You write about the product that you're trying to promote, but without actually referencing the product itself. Instead, you provide links to the product that you're promoting throughout the content of the article. The point of an indirect post is to create curiosity about the product in question.

4. **Comparison Posts:** A comparison post is great because you're able to promote two products at once. You'll want to keep a positive tone for each of the products that you're promoting and highlight both of their features equally.

5. **Special Offer Posts:** These types of posts will offer a coupon or a discount at the end of the read, which will keep the reader engaged throughout the entire article with the hope that they will eventually purchase the product.

As you can see from these different types of posts, an affiliate website is a site that could almost be disguised as a blog. You want to convey the message that you're an expert on whatever it is you're discussing, but keep all of the posts as product-oriented as possible. Without the factor of reputability, consumers are not going to take your affiliate site seriously because it will seem like you're uninformed.

The Type of Products You Should be Recommending

Ideally, you should only be reviewing products on your affiliate website about which you're passionate or familiar. It's likely that consumers are going to know when you're reviewing something that is not personally exciting to you or that is not truly a great product in your eyes. Seek to be as authentic as possible, and your readers are sure to feel this sense of genuineness come through in your posts. This is a good rule to keep in mind for the type of keyword that you're going to be focusing on as well. You want to make sure that you're generally excited about the topic of your website as a whole. Just because a keyword ranks well on Google, it does not 100% mean that you should definitely create a website around it. You should also be passionate about the topic yourself.

Recommending Versus Telling

Another rule that many affiliate marketers swear by is that you should never outright tell people to purchase a product on your site. A better way to get through to people is to recommend what you're selling from the position of personal experience. This will make your online identity more relatable, and will most likely lead to more sales.

Chapter 3: Various Affiliate Marketing Strategies

Depending on the specific affiliate marketing program in which you choose to partake, the parameters of each one could be different. Here we will look at some of the different types of affiliate marketing strategies that exist so that you can find a program that best fits what you're trying to accomplish through your own affiliate marketing presence on the internet.

Type 1: Cost Per Click

When you find a company that will pay you a commission on a "cost per click" basis, this means that whenever someone who visits your site clicks on the link that leads them to the seller's page, you get paid regardless of whether or not they purchase the product.

Type 2: Cost Per Sale

This means that the seller is only going to agree to pay you a commission when your website's link leads to an actual sale. This is considered to be one of the tougher ways to make money through affiliate marketing because there is not much you can do to control whether or not a consumer actually purchases the product after seeing it on your website.

Type 3: Cost Per Lead

For this type of affiliate marketing strategy, the seller is going to pay you whenever the link on your website leads a consumer to sign up to receive emails from the seller in question. Again, this is a more difficult way to earn a commission, because it requires the consumer to do something that is largely out of your control. If you provide an incentive in your own way, this might make it easier to make money from this tactic.

Type 4: Cost Per Action

When you're involved in a program that is cost per action, this means that you're only going to get paid when the consumer completes some predefined action for which the seller is looking. For example, this may mean that you only get paid when the consumer downloads a specific item from the seller's site, or when the consumer completes a survey.

These are the basic types of affiliate marketing programs that are out there. Make sure that you choose to work with a seller who offers the program in which you're most interested, and try not to compromise on what you want until it becomes clear that your options are limited. It's also important that you correspond with many sellers, to get an idea of the types of offers that are out there. Once you find a program, the seller will provide you with programming code that you can embed

into your website. # Chapter 4: Amazon's Affiliate Marketing Program

Amazon's affiliate marketing program, Amazon Associates, is arguably the most popular one on the internet today. Obviously, Amazon is an online marketplace powerhouse that provides millions of products to people all over the world. While you can certainly target smaller businesses when you're looking for products to promote, avoiding Amazon's marketplace would be silly because of its size and capacity for future growth. Below are the steps that you needs to take if you want your website to feature Amazon products.

Step 1: Set up your own website to make it ideal for selling affiliate products

Step 2: Login to your account on Amazon.com. If you want your affiliate account to be separate from your current Amazon account, create a new login prior to continuing. You'll find the "Amazon Associates" link on the menu page for your traditional Amazon account.

Step 3: Once you're in the Amazon Associates portal, click "Join for Free". Next, click "New Customer" and create an Associates account for yourself.

Step 4: Fill out the remainder of the application. This step is pretty similar to applying for any type of service. You'll be required to include your address and contact information. You'll also have to provide your website for review. Amazon wants to make sure that the work that you're already doing on your site will coincide nicely with the products that are available on Amazon. Make sure that you have some content on your website. If your site is empty, Amazon is not going to accept it.

Step 5: Wait for Amazon approval. Once Amazon approves your website, you'll be provided with links that you can embed into your posts and these will lead directly to the Amazon website.

That's it! It's pretty simple to get started with affiliate marketing through Amazon Associates, right?

Chapter 5: Common Mistakes to Avoid

Now that you're aware of the basic concepts surrounding affiliate marketing and have tips to get started, let's take a look at some common mistakes that new affiliate marketers often make. This way, you'll be less likely to make these same mistakes yourself.

Mistake 1: Failure to Cultivate an Email List

If you can promote affiliate products through two platforms, why wouldn't you? You should strongly consider adding a contact page to your website so that you can begin to gather email addresses whenever you can. This way, you can supplement your website's affiliate marketing tactics with email marketing tactics as well.

Mistake 2: Writing Inadequate Reviews

From the perspective of SEO, it's commonly understood that most posts on any reputable website should be at least 2,000 words long. If they're not, it's almost guaranteed that you're going to rank lower on any search engine. Additionally, SEO can also sift through websites and see whether the content is made of quality material or garbage. It's important to take the time that's necessary to write practical and useful articles that will help consumers rather than confuse or frustrate them.

Mistake 3: Not Spending Enough Time Doing Research

The importance of doing keyword research prior to committing to a certain topic cannot be overstated. So many new affiliate marketing enthusiasts disregard the importance of doing sound keyword research prior to developing their site, and this results in utter and complete website failure. If you're not diligent during the research period, you're not going to be able to find a keyword that has a high search volume but low competition. Finding your niche is arguably the most important aspect of developing an affiliate marketing website.

Mistake 4: Forgetting the Importance of Patience

Creating a successful affiliate marketing website requires a lot of patience and dedication. If you're someone who tends to get irritated easily at obstacles, then you're going to want to adjust this attitude prior to starting your affiliate marketing pursuit. Google alone has over 200 credentials that they consider when ranking web pages for SEO, and it's hard to keep track of them all. Google does not publicly state what their SEO principles are, which is why you will have to be patient when figuring out what is going to work for your individual site. Be prepared to go through some periods of trial-and-error, and remember the importance of patience.

PART 2

1. Introduction

Whether you're just breaking into the world of online marketing or you're an expert looking for the latest SEO trends, this book is for you. This book will show you how to make your website stand out from the sea of other similar websites while also honoring the unwritten internet ethical code. Learn (or refresh your memory on) the basics of Search Engine Optimization and see what 2017's trends can do to build up from the basics.

This book won't go in-depth with technological jargon that beginners may not understand. Instead, it will explain the basics of SEO as simply as possible, putting an emphasis on managing content. At the same time, it will take a look at the latest trends relating to content according to the top online marketing experts and list off what they all agree you should use. If you're an expert in online marketing, don't overlook the basic beginner strategies because there's information there that could still apply to you. Just like a little black dress, there are trends in SEO that never go out of style.

While the names and corporations used as examples in this book are fictional, you can learn a lot from what happens to them. Think of it like watching a mockumentary, like *The Office.*

Without further ado, let us begin.

a. Chapter 1: Strategies for Beginners

1. What is an SEO keyword?

SEO stands for "search engine optimization."

Basically, it's a tool to make sure that your website is easy for search engines such as Google to find. The way that search engines work is that they read the content of your website and analyze it, looking for topics and keywords, and puts your page in their index. Then, when someone searches for your site, your page will come up in the search results.

Say that you are a wedding planner and that you have a website advertising your services. If you want your website to be found whenever someone types in "wedding planner" in a search engine, you need to make sure that your website has the word "wedding planner" beyond just the title page. The words need to be in the content of your web page.

What other words will you need if you have a wedding planner website? Here are some keywords:

- a wedding planner list
- wedding planning service
- wedding planner checklist
- wedding planner cost
- wedding planner budget
- wedding planners near me

If you want to find keywords for your website, check out websites like keywordtool.io or wordtracker.com which give you a sample list for free and provides keywords for search engines such as Google, Bing, and Amazon. It also provides keywords for international search engines, which is great if you don't live in the United States.

2. How does Google rank sites?

Google ranks websites based on how relevant and useful they are to whatever is being searched. A search for "wishing well" usually brings up images of a well or the song "I'm Wishing" from Disney's *Snow White* since the words "wishing well" are in the lyrics. The way they determine which websites are most useful and relevant depends on a complex program. However, what most SEOs know for certain is that sites are usually ranked by the following factors:

- how often a certain keyword is used
- the structure of the website
- how fast the website is

- how much time people usually spend on a
  website

Simply put, getting your website to be put first on a Google search depends on content and image. By content, you need to make sure that your website has keywords that relate to what you think people will search for.

3. What works? What doesn't? What's trending?

One current trend that beginners and experts can both do easily is collaborating with other websites and writing guest posts on blogs. This can go beyond two people collaborating on a movie review.

Nonprofit organizations often rely on collaboration

in order to make their projects successful. The Wishing Well is a nonprofit organization that organized fundraising to make their clients' dreams come true, such as aspiring comic book artist Jim Bartlett.

After talking with The Wishing Well, Jim created a website promoting a fundraising event: a special historical tour of his hometown. The Wishing Well wrote an article on Jim's website that contained details of the fundraising event. In that article, they talked a little about themselves, but they gave more attention to Jim's comic and what Jim planned to show in the hometown historical tour. Not only was the tour a success for Jim, but it brought a whole new customer base for The Wishing Well.

Another basic technique you'll need to know is to

understand analytics. Most people use Google Analytics to track how well their website is doing. Google Analytics shows you how many people visit your site every day, what kind of people visit your site, which pages and posts got the most views, and how long people stay on your website. You will need to set up an account on Google in order to use Google Analytics, but it's a worthwhile investment.

Make sure that you and only a handful of trusted people can gain access to the analytics. You don't want anyone hacking into your data. Once you linked Google Analytics to your web page, it will give you a tracking code that you can put on your webpage.

One benefit of Google Analytics is that it can help you keep track of the goals you set for your website.

Let's say that you want a hundred people to subscribe to your website by Christmas. When you go to Google Analytics, you can set up a goal according to whatever milestones you have in mind for your website. Once the goal is set up, Google Analytics will measure your website until that goal has been met.

The most important technique you'll need to know, whether you're a beginner or an expert, is to make sure your content is top quality. Stay relevant and keep a good relationship with your audience. Ask them for feedback. If you're creating a website dedicated to sharing and reviewing mystery books, make sure that your website has quality book reviews of the latest novels from authors such as James Patterson and Michael Connelley.

Take advantage of visual content as well. Just don't put super-large images on your website, as big pictures tend to slow down a webpage's loading time. Trust me when I say that you don't want a slow website. It will drop your website down in the search engine rankings. Just like with pop stars, the popularity of your website will have to look good and make users feel like they can relate to your content.

4. How does SEO work with social media?

When you share your web page on social media platforms such as Facebook or Twitter, make sure that your most important SEO keywords are in the URL (www.exseo.com/important-keyword-here).

Don't limit yourself to just Facebook or Twitter. Try promoting your stuff on Instagram and Pinterest, especially if you're selling a product. Mimi Lu has an

Etsy store where she sells her handmade dolls and stuffed animals and she posts pictures of her products on Instagram since she has a large following.

Make sure that you still include keywords when you post pictures. Mimi usually uses hashtags in her Instagram posts. Her picture of the stuffed bunnies she made for Easter are tagged with #handwork #handmade #handcrafts #sewing, #felt #easterbunny #toys #bunny #crafting. Figure out which hashtags work best for your product and put them below the description.

b. Chapter 2: 2017 SEO Trends For Marketing Experts

1. Going Mobile

Today, more people search for things on their mobile devices than desktop computers. It seems like everyone has a smartphone or a tablet. When it comes to searching for websites on mobile devices, how fast a website is what matters most. If a website is slow to load, potential viewers and customers will be lost.

Accelerated Mobile Pages (AMP) are what your website would look like on a mobile device. AMP eliminates all the unnecessary information of your web page and strips it down to its most basic level.

The good news is that since mobile versions of web pages are so simple, it will make it easy for you to make an AMP version of your website. Just make sure that the mobile version of your website has all the important and relevant information in its content. Structure the content of your site with easy consumption in mind. Use bullet points, lists, and subcategories for fast skimming. If you're writing something that can't be put into a list, keep your paragraphs short.

2. Voice Searching

Have you ever seen commercials where people talk to a digital assistant like Google Home or Amazon Echo? Have you ever used your smartphone to ask

Siri or Cortana for something? Voice searching has become a major contribution to how Google ranks websites.

There are three questions you need to keep in mind when it comes to voice searching. This will especially apply to the mobile-friendly version of your website:

- How will voice searching affect your website's user traffic?

- How can you deliver your content to make sure it comes up in a voice search?

- Does the content of your website use natural language?

Of course, you might be wondering what natural language even is. Think about how you use the voice search app on your mobile device. You don't say "Movie times." You say "What are the movie times for [insert movie here] at [local movie theater] today?" Voice search apps are like journalists. They use "who, what, where, why and how" questions to get results.

This doesn't mean that you should eliminate the usage of keywords. In fact, you'll need to look for longer keyword phrases. Also, keep the questions that your customers are asking in mind. Channel your inner Lois Lane and look for how to answer the "who, what, where, why and how" questions on your website and on social media. When it comes to content, make sure that you write like you were talking to a friend. Your users will feel like they're having a conversation with you and your website will be more likely to pop up in a voice search.

3. Think Local

Take advantage of what's needed in your local town or city. Say that you live in the Texas Hill Country and your town is famous for its antique stores, the bluebonnets that grow every spring, and other seasonal events. When you make a website about your town, highlight what makes your town special all year round. Create a page that highlights the local old fashioned soda shop and artisan bakery. This way, you can promote and support local businesses.

Create a blog that talks about events happening in

your town, like the latest community theater production or an art fair with works created by artists in your town and nearby neighborhoods. Link your website with keywords that are associated with your town's attractions and events. If you're really ambitious, write a book chronicling the history of your town and write about what makes your town special. Texas always supports writers who promote the state's culture and all the things that make Texas unique. See if you can use that in your local community.

4. User Experience Optimization

UEOs are a relatively new subcategory of SEOs, but the fact of the matter is that the two go hand in hand. After all, search engines rely on users. If you want to stay on top of your game and make the most of the UEOs, you need to take user intent into account.

So what exactly are the goals of user intent?

1. Deliver an immediate and useful answer to the user

2. Bring the user to where they need to go most

3. Assist the user in completing a purchase or task.

What do you want your user to do once they arrive on your web page? What is the purpose of your web page and how can you make sure that users will make the most from it? Is your website there to inform users or sell products or a service to users? Why would a user need your website? Once you find the answer to those questions, you can manage the content of your site to make sure that the user gets the information they need right away and at the same time lead them to do whatever you want to get out of them in return.

You need to make sure the site is as efficient and as easy to navigate through as possible. It's all about a business's online perception/presence. Focus on the interaction between your product and the user. Make sure you use stock photos or photos you've taken yourself, make sure that your text is clear and easy to read. Make sure your navigational buttons and links lead users to the right place.

At the same time, you need to make sure that your site still loads as quickly as possible, whether it's on a desktop computer or a mobile device. As stated before, slow loading times will lead to a decrease in your site's rankings. Worst case scenario, your site might be dropped entirely.

5. Consistent, Quality Content

Articles on SEO blogs conflict between small content and long content. The happy medium they can all agree with is having dense, rich, quality content that is put out on a consistent basis. This means that you don't have to add unnecessary information or use a million different keywords to your webpage in order to make sure that your website rises in the search engine rankings. It's enough nowadays to write short articles (say 300-500 words) that are straightforward and full of valuable information. You can still write longer posts, but make sure that there's a good mix of both long and short articles.

What's most important, as always, is the quality of

what you post.

c. **Chapter 3: Ethical Guidelines**

1. What Is The Purpose of Ethics?

Once upon a time, there was a corporation in a big city called Alpha Industries that makes its living trading commodities. It required all its employees to be graded on a scale of 1 to 10, with employees who score a 1 being marked for termination and employees who score a 10 were given a bonus. It was the most cutthroat, ruthless corporation in the whole city. In the eyes of Wall Street, Alpha Industries was a financial darling. What nobody realizes is that the trading company hid a dark secret.

Alpha Industries used their PR division to

create an article about the latest trading news for a partner website. On the surface, it looked like a friendly collaboration. However, the company used the byline to create a link back to the company's website. The company also encouraged its interns to leave comments on business-related online forums and blog posts with links back to the site. Some of them even left links in the comments of YouTube videos that talked about the latest financial news.

Alpha Industries also included paid for links whenever they negotiated with their clients, article directories and blog networks, all designed solely for the purpose of building links. They built websites that linked to their trading partners and companies they sponsored. The PR department put out daily press releases to get links to the company in news websites.

These tactics are referred to in the industry as "black hat techniques." These days, Google has an algorithm that tracks and penalizes sites that use these techniques. Companies like Alpha Industries would have their websites suspended from the search engines. Stick to what the industry calls "white hat techniques" and focus on creating content without oversaturating your website with SEOs and links.

2. The Customer Is Always Right

Whether your business is local or on the Fortune 500 list, a business's reputation with its customer base is basically everything.

A media corporation named KJ Enterprises took over a newspaper of a small town and completely changed the paper's content. The CEO of this media corporation, Kevin Johnson, released clickbait articles and lists that focused on celebrity gossip and scandals. When word got out that he fired the former owners and legacy employees, the townsfolk reacted by unsubscribing to the paper and staged a protest in support of the former newspaper owners and employees who were wrongfully terminated from the company.

You need to make sure that you have a good

relationship with your customer base. Pay attention to the quality of your content and ask your viewers for feedback. You can't force the people who visit your site to write a review, but you can create a page on your site that encourages your customer base to review your business and give you feedback. If your customer reviews are good quality, ask your customers if you can post their reviews on your website.

3. Avoid Copycats

Search engines usually discard web pages that have duplicate content. It's okay if you share your stuff multiple times on social media, but don't make a habit of it. And don't republish your articles on other websites.

If you're selling things on your website, make sure you have a variety of products. Don't just change the product name and image whenever you renew your inventory. Update your website with new information on your products and include customer reviews.

Avoiding duplicate content is a pretty simple step, but it helps to make sure your website is neat and tidy. It helps to have your website audited every year to make sure that you are being consistent in creating top-quality content.

PART 3

Chapter One: How to Gain More Reviews

Reviews are vital to your business on Amazon if you are wanting to sell more product. The more reviews and the better your reviews are, your chances will increase on others buying your product. While it is sometimes hard to believe, more and more people are looking at the reviews on the products that they are wanting to buy off of Amazon so that they can decide if your product is going to be the best one for them to buy or if they should continue looking for someone else who may have the same product but at a lower price.

Customers of Amazon have guidelines that they are required to follow whenever they are leaving a review on the site about a product. Therefore, if you are trying to get reviews from people that you know or by offering discounted or free product to customers on Facebook or through an email promotion, you need to make sure that your customers know what the guidelines are for leaving a review on Amazon so that you are not losing reviews due to someone not putting a review up that met Amazon standards.

Amazon review guidelines:

- You can ask customers that have bought your product before to leave a review by sending them a newsletter or posting something on social media. This is one of the best ways to get an honest review because you already have a customer that has bought your product and apparently likes you because they have subscribed to your newsletter or liked your page on social media.

- Make sure that you are offering excellent customer service. Most bad reviews come from poor customer service due to the fact that they feel as if they are being misled by the product's description or they contact you over an issue, and you do not respond, or you are rude when you do respond.

- After someone has made a purchase, send out a follow-up email to ask them to leave a review of the product that they purchased from you.

- Amazon ranks its top reviewers, and you can solicit the top reviewers by offering them your product in exchange for an honest review. If you are looking for someone that is on the top reviewer's list, you are going to see a title next to their name such as "Top Ten Reviewer" or "Hall of Fame Reviewer."

- Another way to get reviews is to go to the pages that offer a product that is similar to yours and find their reviewers. You may not get the customer to buy your product, but you can learn what you should and should not do with your product so that you can get better reviews than your competitor.

Those are just some of the ways that you can get reviews. There are other ways that you can get reviews but ensure that you are following the rules that Amazon has put into place, or you are going to end up getting reviews taken off of your product due to the fact that the rules that Amazon has put into place for the reviews, no matter what method it is that you are using.

Chapter Two: Strategies to Sell Products on Amazon

Not only are reviews important, but the way that you market your product is important as well. If you do not give the proper description for your product, or you do not provide quality pictures of your product, then you will not find a lot of customers who are going to be willing to purchase your product.

The best method to selling your products is to use Amazon FBA. When trying to sell on Amazon, it is vital to have a strategy on how you are going to sell your product. There is no promise that you are going to sell enough of your product in order to make up for all the money that you will spend in manufacturing it. But, that is the hope correct? Hopefully, through the use of some well-placed strategies, you can not only make up for production costs but also make a profit too.

As you have probably already figured out, the rankings on Amazon work like this. The more sales you get plus, the more reviews your product receives, the higher your ranking is will be on Amazon. But, we are going to go into further detail in that in chapter four so that you can fully understand the ranking system as it applies to Amazon.

The strategies that we are about to discuss are meant to not only help you sell more product but help you to get more reviews so that your Amazon ranking goes up! There are a ton of different tactics that you can use besides the ones that are discussed in this chapter.

- Amazon Ads: if you are selling on Amazon, you need to be using Amazon Ads. Through the use of Amazon ads, your keyword rankings are going to increase because your product is getting more exposure. Amazon ads are only available for sellers on Amazon.

Ads can be accessed through the "Campaign Manager" through the Amazon Seller Central.

It is a good idea to start off with automatic targeting so that your promotion ads reach as many people as possible. Keep in mind, the higher that your daily budget is, the more exposure your ad is going to get. After there have been a couple of hundred dollars in your sales, then you will be able to run your report so you can determine which keywords are being searched the most for people to find your product. From there you are going to set up your manual targeting and use those specific keywords that people are searching in order to find your product online.

- Give away some of your product: this does not mean that you will just be giving away product for free. Instead, you are giving away product for a lower price than what you are attempting to sell it for. Sell it for a dollar or two so that more people become interested in it and buy it.

By offering your product for the cheaper pricing, you are going to sell more products and most likely gain some more reviews which is going to assist you in raising within the rankings of Amazon.

A good way to be sure that millions of people are not just buying your product for a dollar or two is to hand out coupon codes to your friends and family as well as their friends. This will allow them to purchase your product for the lower price and then once they have purchased your product, you will have the ability to confront them and see if they are willing to leave an honest review.

In doing this, you will more than likely break even or risk losing money instead of making money. The primary thing that is going to determine how much money you earn or lose is going to determine how much it costs for you to manufacture your product. So, in order to make sure that you do not lose too much money, you are going to want, to begin with a product that is not expensive to produce.

- Tomoson is a website that will grant you access to the world of thousands of bloggers that are just standing in line to receive your product for a review as well as promotion.

Tomoson allows you to set up a free trial so that you can see how well it works for you. You are going to need to list your product there and then respond to the emails that you are going to get from the bloggers that are excited to help promote your product.

Through this, you are going to be required to give your product to the bloggers for free. But, you can always provide them with a coupon that is going to allow them to get it for a dollar so that you are still getting money and not violating any of Amazon's review rules.

After they have received the item that you have supplied them with to review you are going to want to ensure that they do the following so that you are able to get more eyes on your product.

- o Leave an honest review on Amazon
- o Post the product and their review to their social media pages
- o Post a review on their blog with a link to the Amazon page
- o Create a YouTube video that will link it to Amazon

You will realize that many people are going to be perfectly fine doing all of this for you just to test the product that you are selling. But, there are a few blogs that you will come across that will end up having a fee in place to promote your product. This fee can be as little as five dollars and go as high as fifty.

It is a good idea just to pay the fee if the blog is big enough and will enable a lot of sales from that blog.

- Buview and Zonblast are just another way for you to sell more product and rise through the Amazon ranks.

These resources are going to be aimed towards Amazon sells in order to help with the promotion and sale of your product on other people's lists. This can end up meaning that you have to "give away" products but, even if you just use coupon codes, there is a likelihood that you are going to get a decent return.

A major drawback is that you are going to have to pay money to use services such as Buview and Zonblast, but if you do not have it in your budget to do so, you are not required to use these services. It just another strategy that you can use in order to improve your sales.

Keep in mind that you are going to need to reserve a significant amount of your stock before you purchase these services or else your inventory is going to quickly be wiped out. You will need to closely monitor your inventory so that you know exactly how many items you are giving away or selling through the use of these services.

- Last but not least there is always Facebook; you can use Facebook ads as well as fan pages that will help you pull customers and sell products.

Chapter Three: Strategies for Getting Product from Suppliers

Having a relationship with your vendors is important because they are going to be your partners. Suppliers are going to be the people that help support you when you are trying to get the goods that you need for your products.

The suppliers are going to be the people that will advise you with information as well as assist in evaluating any new items that you may potentially be wanting to sell. Suppliers also contribute in identifying design flaws and offering ideas on how you can improve these weaknesses so that you are able to cut costs and sell more product than your competition.

It is easy to try and go with the first supplier that

offers you a good deal; however, you are not going to want to do that. You are going to want your supplier to help you grow rather than stay stagnant. Having a good relationship with your supplier leads to improved service that you receive from that vendor's company. By improved service I mean that the supplier is going to tell you what does not work for you and your company, you will receive discounts on the supplies that you need, and ultimately it leads to a better buyer/ supplier relationship.

In order to create a good relationship with your vendor you will want to:

- Know the lingo by learning the basics of the industry. That way you can show your vendor that you are open to learning but that you are going to advocate for yourself on the deals that you get with your vendor.

- Do not compromise on communication.

- Look up what the actual costs are so that you can better negotiate a price.

- Think like the supplier. They want to sell you something, and you want to buy it so that you can sell it. Therefore, you will want to show that you are a resource to that vendor's company instead of a risk.

Chapter Four: Understanding the Ranking System on Amazon

Your product's ranking on amazon is going to determine how many potential customers see that product when they are browsing the Amazon website. The higher the ranking for your product is, the more people are going to see it. So, what you are going to want to do is raise your Amazon ranking so that your product is seen over your competition's product.

- Your ranking is going to be dependent on the search bar. How often does a customer search for your particular product? The search bar is one of the biggest factors in your ranking because this is where all of the customers look for the products they want to see.

- Keep your product title under sixty characters.

- Use the bullet points Amazon offers so that your customer can see what they need to see about the product such as dimensions of the product.

- Be descriptive about your product! Your product description is what sells your product.

- Do not skip over the keywords. These keywords are going to assist in customers locating your product so that they can buy it rather than buying your competition's product.

Your ranking on Amazon can also go up if you use an ASIN, the ASIN is going to make it to where you can compete in prices, but you are going to be placing your product on someone else's post as a way to try and redirect the customer so that they come to your product page rather than the one that they are currently on. This means that you have to offer your product for a lower price, even if that price is a penny less than what the competition is offering theirs for.

Chapter Five: Products – The Good, The Bad, and The Ugly

Having a good product to sell on Amazon is going to make it to where you can make a profit off of Amazon. However, there are also going to be products that you are not going to want to sell on Amazon. It is vitally important that you know the difference between the products that you want to see and the products that you are going to want to be away from.

When you look through Amazon, you see that just about everything can be sold on Amazon. While this is great, that does not mean that you need to sell whatever on Amazon, you are going to want to stick to the products that are going to push you through the ranking system while making you a profit and having customers coming back for more.

- The product you offer should be light so that you are saving yourself the headache of a product being damaged when it is shipped. This will also save on shipping costs and even customs costs if it is being shipped overseas.

- Ensure that your product is easy to manufacture so that you are leaving less room for error in the production of the product. You want your product to be high quality.

- Try and keep your product under two hundred dollars. There is going to be a greater risk to you if you are selling a product that is going to cost more than two hundred dollars because you are taking on a greater risk and that product will most likely require a higher level of quality control.

- Stay away from the products that you would buy. If it is something that everyone buys, go the other way with your product so that you do not have to compete with the big box stores where a customer is going to be able to go to get the product right away rather than wait for it to be shipped.

- Seasonal stuff is great to sell, but you are going to end up not having any sales the rest of the year. If you are going to do something seasonal, then make sure you have other products to sell as well it also helps keep excessive inventory down.

- Some products have to have warranties on them if they break down, try and steer clear of these products so that you are not losing money in replacing parts that may have broken in shipping. This will also make sure that you are not opening yourself up to a lawsuit.

- Lastly, trademarks are going to end up getting you sued in the event that you do not obtain the proper permission needed to sell it. But, keep in mind, if you buy it from overseas, it is most likely not an authentic product.

With this list, you are going to have a decent place to start when it comes to selling product on Amazon and what you should stay away from.

PART 4

INTRODUCTION

Before we get into the different types of passive income, let's first talk about what it actually is. Passive income is money that is earned from a source in which he or she is not physically involved. Like active income, passive income is taxed, though it is usually treated a little differently by the Internal Revenue Service (IRS). States differ slightly in their tax laws, so make sure to see a certified public accountant before filing your taxes with the IRS.

Overall, there are three types of income. Passive, which is the subject of this e-book, active and portfolio income. To give a little insight into the difference between the three, we will briefly outline active and portfolio income before delving into different types of passive income.

Although it should seem self-explanatory, we are going to detail what active income is. Active income is a job that requires the earner to be physically present. In the United States, the most common forms of active income are hourly and salary. Hourly employees earn a wage for each hour they work while salary employees are paid a flat rate regardless of how many hours they put in. Most companies pay weekly or biweekly, although there are a few who pay monthly. However, those tend to be government or teaching positions.

Surprisingly enough, freelance work is also considered active income. The person in the freelance position gets paid for work upon its completion. One of the downfalls of freelance work is if you are sick or unable to complete a project, there is no paycheck. Writing articles, e-books and traditional books and photography are the most common types of freelance jobs.

Portfolio income is money earned from royalties, investments, capital gains and dividends. For tax purposes, the IRS does not consider portfolio income to be passive income as it does not come from traditional businesses or passive investments.

Now that we have talked about the different types of income let's talk about why passive income is a great way to earn extra money for savings, retirement, vacations or anything else you would like to spend your money on.

While you should be very excited about what we will learn in this book, it is important to note that passive income does not mean 'easy money.' Like all other forms of income, there is some work involved whether it is research, development, writing an e-book or selling photographs online. Wouldn't turning a hobby into income be an excellent way to earn some extra money? One of the ways we will discuss in this book is exactly that. Even using a hobby to earn a passive income takes some time and effort up front, although it is probably the most enjoyable of all the forms of passive income, we will cover in this book.

If you have some time and energy to devote to passive income from the comfort of your own home (maybe even in your pajamas while you sip coffee), let's talk about some of the exciting ways you can earn a passive income!

Chapter 1

Surveys, Selling Photos

& Teaching Classes

Surprisingly enough, there are lots of ways to make money on the internet. We will list some of the more passive ways to earn money online and then give you some insight into how you can get going with passive income online.

Websites like InboxDollars actually pay people to shop online, play games and even search the web. InboxDollars has been around since 2000, and the company itself employs thirty people. They offer anywhere between 1-10 cents per email read and the payment on playing games or going to an affiliate website varies. As with any web-based income potential, there are pros and cons to InboxDollars. The first payment isn't sent until you've earned thirty bucks. At that, it can take up to two weeks to receive payment so if you are looking for quick and easy, InboxDollars isn't the place to be. However, if you are hanging out in front of a computer while sipping on a latte at your local coffee shop, why not sign up and earn some money simply for surfing the net or reading emails? You are already online anyway, right?

Another site similar to InboxDollars is called **SwagBucks.** InboxDollars website is a little easier to maneuver, and they categorize each option for earning cash online. SwagBucks does require you to sign up with them before you can see the earning potential. Swagbucks doesn't pay in cold, hard cash. They pay in the form of "SwagBucks," which is their term for earning points. Each SwagBuck is approximately one cent. That means once you've accrued one-hundred, you've made roughly one dollar. SwagBucks are redeemable for gift cards only. There are no checks or payments sent to your PayPal account. As opposed to InboxDollars, SwagBucks will actually pay you for referrals, in the form of their SwagBucks, of course. For every survey your referral completes, you get ten percent. That's actually a great deal considering it is someone else doing the work, right? One last thing to mention about these websites. They both pay you to sign up for trial offers, which is something you need to be very careful with. While they both will pay a pretty decent amount for your signing up, you have to remember to cancel your membership within the month, or your credit card will be charged for the service. Of the two, Swagbucks pays more; usually enough to earn a twenty-five dollar gift card, which is actually a fantastic deal!

In addition to earning a passive income by signing up for websites like those mentioned previously, you can also sell your photography online. Obviously, this is geared toward those who enjoy taking photos as a hobby. As it isn't for everyone, we will discuss it briefly before moving onto the next subject.

If you do enjoy taking photos of scenic overlooks, nature, or even people (with their permission of course), you can sell your photos to places like Shutterstock and Stock photo. Depending on which site you choose, they will pay either with a percentage of overall sales of your photo or a flat fee for each photo that is sold to the client. One of the great things about selling your photos is one picture can earn money more than once. Each time it is sold, you'll get a percentage (or the aforementioned flat fee). If you always liked photography but hadn't really given it a second thought, maybe now is the time to do so. You do have to go out and take the pictures, but it is a great way to get some exercise, fresh air, see some awesome sights and earning some of that passive income!

Another way to earn passive income is to write an e-book. Like photography, it has to be something that you have an interest in. Since it isn't everyone's cup of tea, we'll go over it briefly, just like we did with photography.

There are several ways to make money with writing e-books. Fiction, fantasy, how-to, cookbooks...the list is endless. There is some work up front, and if you aren't the best with commas and periods, it might be prudent to hire an editor just to make sure you don't miss anything major. Some of the most popular books are how to and fantasy. If you are particularly knowledgeable on a subject, or you have an incredibly active imagination, either of those would be an excellent way to start earning passive income.

Once the book is written, you can publish it on Amazon and wait for some money to start coming in. If you want to make decent money, you will want to invest some time in marketing. This is something you can do yourself using your already established social media outlets. Facebook, Twitter, and Instagram are great for free advertising.

Did you know that you can make money by posting YouTube videos online? This too takes some work and a bit of marketing on your part, but once you get going who knows? Maybe you will be the next YouTube sensation! As we outlined with writing an e-book, there are several areas in which you can create a YouTube channel. Book or restaurant reviews, music, opinions, comedy, music and tutorials of all kinds including hair, makeup, rebuilding engines or fixing just about anything around the house. From sinks to refrigerators, people are always looking for a way to fix things themselves so that they don't have to spend thousands of dollars hiring someone to come out to their house and take care of it for them. The key to success with this type of internet income is marketing. We already talked about those social media outlets in the e-book section. You can utilize those to market your YouTube videos as well. Making the video itself is not as easy as it sounds, but it can be quite a bit of fun. There will be some trial and error; and once it's done there will be some editing involved, but it is free to post videos to YouTube meaning no upfront cost. You'll only need to put the time and energy into creating your YouTube masterpiece.

The last topic we'll go over for internet income is creating an online course or an online guide. Is there something that you are particularly great at? Perhaps you know a lot about medieval history, how to rebuild a transmission for a particular or rare car, or maybe you can teach people how to sell real estate. Really, whatever you are good at and/or passionate about, you can create a course to help others who might be looking to expand their own knowledge base.

While there are a few platforms in which you can do this, one of the best-known platforms is Udemy.com. They have over *eight million* students looking to learn something new every day. That is a huge number of people to whom you can sell your product. What's great about this is there isn't a whole lot you need to do in the way of marketing. Udemy has it all categorized. You would want to write a killer description of your tutorial, though. That way, you would have a bit of an advantage over others who might be teaching related online courses. This is literally something you can make money at while you sleep. Your course can include a video, tutorials, lessons and checklists. What's great about Udemy is you can make it your own. There are even several price points for this website meaning you can have a higher price point that has all the bells and whistles and then lower price points that have a little less, but still the same great information you are providing at the higher price. This makes it so you can market to a larger group of people maximizing your potential for passive income.

Finally, you can make an online guide. Again, the possibilities here are endless. You can create a guide to the best fishing in the country, white water rafting, skiing...whatever you'd like. Online guides don't usually cost anything to the person searching for those items. Where you make your money with guides is through advertisers. If you are creating a guide to fishing, you'd want to check with bait shops and any outdoorsy type retail place that would want to place an ad on your site. Some pay by the click, others pay if someone purchases something through their website after clicking from your guide. It depends on the retailer, but this is a great way to earn passive income. What's not to love about sharing your expertise and making money in the process?

We've covered quite a few things in this opening chapter! We have outlined just a few of the ways you can earn a passive income using the internet. One of the best things about the things we talked about is they can be fun, especially if writing or photography is a hobby. Taking surveys probably isn't how you picture yourself spending your weekend, but when it comes to passive income, you have to admit that clicking through a survey or getting paid to play a new online game is pretty passive. That being said, there are much more ways and exploring those is just a Google search away. Find something that interests you and the sky is the limit.

Chapter 2 – Passive Income Earned From Investing

Investing may sound daunting. It's highly likely you are looking to passive income as a way to make money because you don't have a lot of excess cash laying around. Let's face it...the majority of us don't. While investing may sound intimidating and expensive, rest assured there are ways to earn a passive income without having to put a second mortgage on your house or dip into your children's college funds.

One of the first things you can look at in the way of investing is joining a Lending Club. This is a web-based lending program geared toward peer to peer borrowing and lending. Unlike traditional investing in US Treasury Securities or bank certificates, Lending Clubs offer a much higher yield on returns. Bonds and other bank certificates usually earn about one-percent which is passive income in the basest of terms. Making that little every year won't do much in the way of helping you retire sooner or get to that beach house you've been looking to vacation at for the past few years. Lending Clubs have a much higher interest rate and with that comes an increased risk. Like bank loans, those given through a Lending Club are at risk of default meaning if the borrower doesn't repay the note to you, that's money you've just lost on investment.

The risk of a defaulted loan is minimal if you know what kinds of loans are more likely to be paid back. For example, you wouldn't want to invest in a mom and pop coffee shop that is slotted for location in the midst of several big chain coffee shops. While that is a risk that can pay off, it might be a little too risky for your liking. And that's okay! When it comes to investing, you have to do what makes you comfortable. Especially when we are talking about putting up some of your own, hard-earned money. Remember, the thought of doing that might make you a little uneasy, but the payoff can be very rewarding.

Lending Clubs usually recommend you start out with an initial deposit of around 2500.00. You can invest as little as twenty-five dollars on a single loan, meaning you can actually invest in up to one-hundred businesses at a time. The potential for earning passive income using this method is higher, and you are invested in businesses that you didn't have to put all your blood, sweat and tears into starting up. That's pretty passive and far less stressful. The beautiful thing about Lending Clubs is there are several that are free to join. That's great if you know a good chunk of what you do have saved is going to go to the initial deposit.

In terms of investing, you can also look into Index Funds. It is a form of mutual fund that helps you to invest in the stock market in an entirely passive manner. These is especially great because you don't have to concern yourself with choosing an investment, knowing when to buy or sell, or rebalancing your portfolio. All of those things are handled by the index fund.

One of the best sites to set up an index fund is Scottrade. Their website is easy to maneuver, setting up an account is pretty affordable. Their website offers levels of investment and depending on how much you invest; you'll also be rewarded with a minimum of fifty free trades. It's a pretty awesome deal. Not to mention, you get to choose where your money goes. Also, if you set up with Scottrade and decide to invest in a different manner, you'll already have an account established with them. Along the same lines as investing, if you are looking to get a retirement fund going (outside of a traditional 401k you may have through your full-time job), Roth IRA's are a great place to put your money. And, if you leave your job you can roll your 401k into a

Roth IRA without having to pay huge tax penalties.

Another way to invest online is the use of a Robo-advisor. If you are worried about trying to decipher stocks and how the market works, let a Robo-advisor do the job for you. One Robo-advisor that gets some of the best reviews is Betterment. You provide them with the funds, and their algorithms will find the best investments for you. In addition to that, it will keep your portfolio balanced. Talk about passive! While there is the upfront cost of investing, you won't have to stress over reading the paper or watching the news every day to see where your stocks are at.

One of the most well-known and popular ways of investing is in the Real Estate Market. As with most investments, this can come with some risk, and there are more ways to invest in Real Estate than just flipping houses or turning them into rental properties. Because rental properties are the most common, we will discuss them in a little greater detail.

Real Estate rentals aren't entirely passive income

makers. There is some work involved in finding the house or apartment complex, but once you've found a property and rented it out, you'll only need to make sure your tenant sends you a rent check every month. You can also hire property management companies to manage your rental for you. Their typical fee is approximately ten-percent of the rental amount every month. One of the benefits of rental properties is once the original loan is paid off, your earnings go up substantially. If you have more than one property that's paid off and bringing in decent rent each month, you might even be able to retire and turn your investments into full-fledged passive income.

Along the same lines, you can also invest in Real Estate Investment Trusts, also known as REITs. As previously mentioned, investing in real estate itself isn't entirely passive. However, if you want to invest in real estate completely passively, REITs are the way to go. This is kind of like investing in a mutual fund with various real estate projects as opposed to stocks or bonds. Like mutual funds, REITs are managed by professionals, so you won't have to worry about learning all the legalities of real estate. REITs pay a higher dividend than most bonds, stocks or even bank investments. You can also sell your REIT at any time making it a more fluid form of passive income since you'll never actually have to invest in an actual property.

There is one final note we'll mention in regards to real estate. If you already own your own home and have some space available, you can rent out that unused space on Airbnb. It's a relatively new concept, but over the past year, it has exploded all around the globe. This engine allows people to travel all over the world and stay places much cheaper than hotels, hostels or traditional bed and breakfasts. By signing up for Airbnb, you can earn money simply by renting out your unused space to travelers. Obviously, there is some risk involved, but Airbnb has a community safety and standards expectations for people renting their space as well as those seeking places to stay. A form of government-issued identification is required so there isn't much to worry about in the way of hosting a felon. The site provides income examples, and a relatively easy search showed that one room in Denver, Colorado can go for as much as 250.00 per week. Not bad for passive income and the best part about this is, you already *own* the investment property.

Chapter 3 – Start a Blog

There are many things you can do with a blog, but we'll focus on two. Creating your own and buying an existing blog. Creating your own won't be entirely passive, but once again, it is easier than finding a part-time job. And with most passive income internet based ventures, you can do this from the comfort of your couch. You aren't going to miss out on cherished family time or dinner because you had to go from your full-time job to the part-time job.

The trick to blogging is consistency. Thousands of blogs are created every year, and the majority of them are abandoned within a few months. Blogging is a competitive market and if it is something you choose to do, remember to stay consistent, post on a regular basis, market using other social media sites we've discussed previously. Passive income from blogging comes mostly from advertisements. Those big-time advertisers are looking for blogs that get a lot of traffic to advertise their product. This will require some work at the beginning with posting, marketing and reaching out to advertisers to get them to pay you to advertise on your blog. If you like to write, or you have an idea for something that's funny tech savvy, or just completely different, blogging is a great way to earn that semi-passive income.

To be clear, one can't expect to make decent passive income by writing and publishing any old blog. In my quest to find what people are most interested in reading about, I came across a list of a whopping *eighty-one* ideas for writing a blog that will sell. We won't be covering all, but I'm going to list the top ten.

1. **Self-improvement and Self-hypnosis**. Whether you go into a bookstore or are looking for books online, self-improvement is one that piques a lot of people's interest. No one is perfect, and most people are looking for a way to improve themselves. Whether it'd be through physical

fitness or having a more positive attitude in life, there are literally hundreds, if not thousands of self-improvement topics to blog about. Self-hypnosis is incredibly interesting. It isn't what you think, either. We've all seen the silly reality shows where people using hypnosis make their subjects act out of sorts. Self-hypnosis in this context actually goes hand in hand with self-improvement. Self-hypnosis is about meditating your way to a different you. Whether you need to boost your self-esteem or work on confidence and overall outlook on life, self-hypnosis is something that people are highly interested in.

2. **Health and Fitness for Busy People**. This is kind of along the same lines as self-improvement. Many people want to get in better shape, but who really has the time? A blog about fitness for people who are always on the go (and not working on earning passive incomes like we are) would be a great target audience. Plus, many sports and activity retailers would love to pay to advertise on

a site that is suggesting people get into shape. Everything they need to attain their goals is a click away...from *your* blog.

3. **Language and Learning Blogs**. These can be lumped in with creating that online course we discussed earlier. As a matter of fact, should you choose to teach a course, you could include blogs from your personal site as part of the learner's course and content. The language might be a little more difficult if you are only fluent in one, but learning new things always appeals to people.

4. **Earning extra money**. Who better to write a blog about this subject than you? You're well on your way to earning passive income without having to get a second job, right? There are quite a few blogs that discuss passive income, but there aren't many that detail trials, tribulations, and successes. It'd be a nice little niche for you to slide right into.

5. **Food blogs**. We aren't talking about the local pub or fast food chain. Specialty or unique/rare foods

are what interests people. "Foodie" blogs come and go, but the same applies here as it did with fitness. Rating food and restaurants in a way that gets people to read your blog over others will entice advertisers to pay for space on your blog. And, you get to go out and try all kinds of amazing new foods. Sounds like a win-win situation.

So, we've talked about creating your own blog, but what if you aren't interested in writing them yourself? Perhaps you don't quite have the time to invest in doing some research and writing the blog, then finding advertisers for your site. That's okay; there is another way to earn a passive income by purchasing a pre-existing blog. The interesting thing about this idea is all the content is there. You will have to put some effort into maintaining the site, but all the bare bones are set up for you.

A lot of blogs use Google AdSense, which is what provides a monthly income for a blogger. It is based on the ads Google places on their site or blog. Blogs tend to sell for approximately twenty-four times their average monthly income. For instance, if a blog earns two-hundred and fifty dollars per month, the most you'll pay for that blog is three-thousand dollars. Like we mentioned in the chapter about investing in real estate, some things will require a bit of money up front. If you are able to afford this route with buying a blog, keep in mind that if the site is generating two-fifty per month, you will earn your money back in a year. After that, the blog will be making money that will be all profit. With a little effort put into the blog to make sure content remains up to date, it'll be mostly passive and something you can do in your spare time.

Chapter 4 – Selling Products Online

There are a couple of ways to make money by selling products online to earn a passive income. Actually, there are several, but the point of this book is passive income, so we will stick to discussing two great ways to make that money using a website. Drop ship products for another retailer, or sell your own products online. If you don't want to invest a lot of money in products to stock your online store, drop shipping might be more appealing. In this chapter, we will cover both so you can get a good idea as to what will work best for you and fit into your budget.

Drop shipping isn't entirely passive, but it's one of the closest things you can to do earn that passive income. What is it, you ask? Drop shipping is where a product goes directly from the manufacturer to the customer.

And, where do you fit into this equation? You would be the middle man. Drop shipping requires a little effort in that you'd need to set up a website to sell a product. What's particularly significant about this is, you don't have to spend the time creating a product, then marketing it online, calculating sales, paying people to help you out...none of that. The middle man in this scenario simply has the product on their site, and when people arrive to purchase, the order is either automatically or manually forwarded to the manufacturer. The product is then "drop shipped" to the customer. This means you will never have to get your hands dirty. The passive income part of this scenario comes from your earning a percentage of the sales of whatever product or products you have on your website.

In addition to simply being the middle man, let's talk about some other benefits to using drop shipping as your passive income source. One of the biggest advantages is that the startup for this is minuscule, especially compared to some of the other things we've mentioned such as real estate and purchasing a blog. You will also be able to offer an extensive selection and wide variety of products without ever having to purchase the product, store it, then pay to have it shipped to the customer.

The risk is reduced tremendously with drop shipping. Most retailers who set up a website and sell the product have to invest hundreds or even thousands of dollars up front to build their inventory. Drop shipping requires you purchase the product only briefly, then have it shipped directly to the customer. The upfront cost of drop shipping is pretty minimal. You also don't need to worry about renting space to house the product. The store you own is virtual which means you can run your drop ship business from the comfort of your own home. Or, anywhere that has wifi.

What's important to mention about drop shipping is if you want to be successful, you'll need to find a specialized niche. In order to do well with drop shipping, you'll want to do a little research and find retailers that utilize that service. Don't narrow yourself to one or two markets. In the beginning, start small, but the more you are able to expand and the more products you are able to add to your website, the more likely you are to earn a pretty decent passive income.

When it comes to selling your own products on the internet, the possibilities are endless. Online, you can sell any service or product that you can think of. It could be anything from a product you've created, things of a digital nature like software or DVDs, even instructional videos if you have them. If not, this is a great opportunity for you to create them, as discussed in the section regarding Udemy or YouTube videos.

If you don't have want to setup your own website, you can work with affiliates who are willing to sell your product for you. In this instance, it would be like your partner is the drop shipper or middle man and you are the retailer. Either way is perfectly acceptable and a great way to earn a passive income.

How much money you make depends on how much time you are willing to commit to this venture. One story that is particularly intriguing is that of a woman who was able to quit her job and earn one-hundred thousand dollars a year with her online store. Now, let's be clear that this isn't the norm. The reason she was able to make so much money was that she'd found that special niche. Her online store specializes in making handkerchiefs for special occasions like weddings. They don't just produce handkerchiefs, though. They make linen party favor bags, lace umbrellas, pillowcases and much more. That is the kind of idea that will earn significant money. Get those wheels in your head spinning! Undoubtedly you've had some magnificent ideas for products that are unique or even those that would simplify your daily life.

Along these lines, you can also set up a website to sell products that you are familiar with. This is similar to selling your own product except you don't have to create a product...you'll be selling someone else's product. With this concept, you could start out small with one or two products, and after a while, you can add other products that are closely related to what you've already begun to sell. You'd want to make the products similar to avoid needing a large website to sell hundreds of products.

Keeping your site neat, clean and straightforward will bring more traffic.

Chapter 5 – Affiliate Marketing

When it comes to passive income, the majority of people who get into it start out in affiliate marketing. While the concept has been around for quite some time, it became popular after the 4-Hour Work Week was released. Ever since then, people have been excited to find a way to "make money while they sleep." The idea behind affiliate marketing is you earn a commission by promoting other people's products. You make money when a sale is completed thanks to your marketing. This relies heavily on revenue sharing, which can go either way. That means that if you have a product and are looking to sell more of it, you can offer promoters financial incentive for marketing your product. Alternatively, if you do not have a product of your own, you can still make money by promoting a product you believe in or are familiar with.

In this chapter, we are going to get into detail as to what affiliate marketing is and how you can get started earning passive income by using it.

Conversely, there are three or four sides to affiliate marketing, depending on which definition you are looking at. For all intents and purposes, when it comes down to it, there are really only two sides to this marketing equation. There are the product seller and creator on the one hand and the marketer on the other. In affiliate marketing, you can be both the creator and the marketer and profit from 'shared' revenue.

Let's take a closer look at all the working parts of what makes affiliate marketing such a successful venture.

There is the merchant, who can also be the creator, seller, retailer, brand or vendor. Ultimately, the merchant is the creator of the product. For example, Dyson vacuum cleaners. On a smaller scale, it can be a person who creates and sells online courses to people wishing to further their education without having to go back to college. From the solo entrepreneur to online startup companies and even Fortune 500 companies, just about anyone can be the merchant who is behind the affiliate marketing system. The merchant doesn't have to be actively involved. They only have to be able to offer a product to sell.

The next party is the affiliate who is also sometimes referred to as the publisher. Like the merchant, the affiliate can be an entire company or an individual. The affiliate is where the marketing happens. They are the party responsible for promoting one or several products in an attempt to attract and even convince those potential customers that the product is needed or of great value and the customer winds up purchasing this product because of the marketing. One way this type of marketing is achieved is by a review of the product being sold with a blog. Really, this can be done on any social media outlet and Facebook is getting to be a huge platform for affiliate marketing. Perhaps you hadn't noticed it before, but you likely will now. Maybe one of your friends posted something about a product they liked. If you went to that website and bought a product, your friend might have been compensated and would be the affiliate.

Now, while there are two parties to the actual functionality of affiliate marketing, there is one key component to recognize, and that is the customer. Without people to consume the product, there would be no need for affiliate marketing, right?

The consumer or customer might be unaware that they are involved in affiliate marketing. That depends on how the affiliate markets the product. Some affiliates let their customers know up front that they are trying to sell a particular product. Others are more passive in using ads or links in their blogs for people to follow to certain websites. No matter how the consumer gets to the product, the affiliate is paid a commission if there is a sale, so long as there is an agreement between the affiliate and the merchant. Nine times out of ten, there is some sort of arrangement between the two parties. Most people don't tend to push a product without having an incentive to do so. Whether the affiliate gets paid in free product or cold hard cash is something to be worked out between the marketer and affiliate. If you choose to be an affiliate for a product to earn passive income, make sure your contract is clear so that no matter which form of payment is received, you will actually be compensated for your time and effort in marketing the product.

At the beginning of this chapter, we talked about three to four components to affiliate marketing. Because most people only see three true components, we will not go into too much detail with the fourth. However, it should be mentioned, albeit briefly.

The fourth component is the network. In most cases, the network acts as an intermediary between the merchant and the affiliate. The network tends to handle payment between the merchant and the affiliate. They can also be responsible for shipping and delivery of the product being sold. The use of a network is not required, although some bigger corporations tend to use the networks to promote, ship and deliver their product. A good example of a network is Amazon. That website sells everything you can think of from tools and books to toys and household items. They have an Amazon Associate program that allows you to promote any item you sell on their platform. Of course, Amazon charges a fee for this, though it is usually pretty minimal.

Now, there are four simple steps to becoming either a merchant or an affiliate. Most people begin with affiliate because it is slightly easier than starting out as a merchant. We will provide you with the four steps for each so that you can make an informed decision as to which route you'd prefer to take to start earning your passive income.

Becoming an Online Merchant in 4 steps:

1. You need to have an idea for a product. This is tough because many people have it in their head that coming up with an idea is hard, which isn't necessarily true. What happens with most people is they have an idea that they are in love with and that is where the problem is. They become too focused on that *one* idea. To get started as a merchant, you'll want to find products out there

that are already selling well, but that the market isn't already flooded with. You need something that people will want to buy and will be able to use on a daily basis. Perhaps you have an idea that will make household chores easier or a product that can clean as well as bleach without all the toxic fumes. Take a little bit of time and do some research on Google to find ideas or products you can get behind.

2. The second step is to validate your idea. You wouldn't want to make or back a product without knowing that there would be reasonable interest for people to purchase it. Ask family, friends, work associates...anyone you know will be *honest* with you about the product you are looking to sell. Sometimes, that can be tough with family and friends because they want to support you in your ventures. Make sure you are asking people you know will tell you the absolute truth.

3. Create your product or prepare to market the already established product you've decided to sell. Creating products can be costly up front. However, if you've done research, had plenty of people tell you they'd definitely buy it and you are passionate about it, go for it!

4. Finally, once your product is ready, you'll need to find the affiliates willing to sell and market your product on your behalf.

Becoming an Online Affiliate in 4 steps:

1. First and foremost, start reviewing the products in your chosen niche. You can do this via YouTube, a blog or live streams on a platform like Periscope.

2. Collect emails so that you can connect with your audience.

3. Check out joint venture webinars. It is a great platform to make a lot of sales in a shorter period of time. At the same time, you'll be growing your email list and expanding your customer base.

4. Finally, once you get your affiliate business to a point where it is making money you can scale growth by using pay per click advertising.

To recap, there are two ways to get into affiliate marketing; becoming an affiliate or becoming a merchant. With what we've outlined here today, I'm positive you'll be able to find which route works best for you. Perhaps you'll discover you can do both!

Chapter 6 – Venture Capitalism

Investopedia defines venture capitalism as a person who provides capital for startup ventures or one who supports small companies that want to expand but lack access to equities markets. Venture capitalists are people who are willing to invest in these companies because they know they will earn significant returns on the companies if they are successful. There is some risk in investing in companies that are in the startup phase because most new businesses fail within the first year. If it is a risk you are financially able to take, it's an easy way to earn a passive income. The venture capitalist provides the money up front, and when the business succeeds, they get to sit back and relax while the money rolls in.

While there are several paths to becoming a venture capitalist, there are two that are most common and, quite frankly, the simplest to get into. Serial entrepreneurship and tech-oriented investment banking.

The serial entrepreneur differs from a typical entrepreneur in that they will come up with an idea for business, get it started, and then hand the reigns over to someone else. An entrepreneur that is not serial will start a business, get it through the first year and beyond and stick with it until they retire or sell the business. Typically, they do not start more than one business whereas a serial entrepreneur will do this several times throughout their business life. This is ideal for people who have lots of great ideas and want to share them with the world. Once the business is up and running, the serial entrepreneur will earn a passive income from all the businesses they get started. Like many forms of passive income and as we've mentioned a time or two, getting on the road to passive income will take some work. Ultimately, when you are earning money without having to leave your home, whatever you put into the idea, in the beginning, will clearly be worth it.

In addition to the ability to spot a great investment from a mile away, a serial entrepreneur is also great at motivating people and inspiring others to follow them. They are willing to take a personal and business risk. They have the ability to recognize a great market to invest in consistently. Some people have made their career being a serial entrepreneur. Realistically, you could help several businesses get their start, which would not be passive. However, once those businesses are up, running and making good money, all you have to do is sit back and enjoy the fruits of your labor. And that, my friend, is the definition of passive income.

The second is the tech-oriented investment banker. Of the two, this is becoming less common because the risk associated is higher. An investment banker, in general, is someone who provides the capital for business...any business. Now, as we have mentioned previously, for this section, we are specifically talking about tech-oriented investments. These tend to be a little less risky because of the way technology is evolving. People are always looking for the next new, really impressive technological advancement. For this type of venture capitalism, you would invest in some kind of emerging technology, and when it succeeds, you will get to reap the rewards of getting in on this investment on the ground floor. As we have talked about previously, finding a specific niche or even an area of technology in which you are particularly well versed is a great way to keep your risk a little lower. That being said, you probably would not want to invest in several tech companies right away. The point of passive income is earned money with less stress than having to go out and find a part-time job. Do a little research on emerging technologies and find the one you are most confident in.

As we've gone over a few times so far, any kind of investing comes with risk. Of the two most common forms of investing through venture capitalism, you are more likely to succeed and experience less risk with serial entrepreneurship. That being said, if you are very tech savvy and can recognize a great product easily, go that route. Remember, you are trying to get yourself to a point where you are earning that passive income, and that means finding exactly what is going to work best for you.

Conclusion

Thank for making it through to the end of *Affiliate Marketing: Build Your Own Successful Affiliate Marketing Business from Zero to 6*

Figures.

The next step is to start thinking about creating an affiliate website, and from there doing sound keyword research within the topic in which you're interested. Remember, when you're doing keyword research it's important to find a topic that has a high volume of searches, but a low volume of competition in terms of other competitor affiliate sites. Once you find a keyword that works within these parameters, begin to build a site around your findings. Be sure to check out Amazon's Associates affiliate marketing center and make sure that your website is fully adhering to their guidelines. This will provide you with the easiest route to affiliate marketing success as quickly as possible.

About The Author

Hi there it's Jonathan Walker here, I want to share a little bit about myself so that we can get to know each other on a deeper level. I grew up in California, USA, and have lived there for the better part of my life. Being exposed to many different people and opportunities when I was young, it made me want to strive to become an entrepreneur to escape the rat race path that most of my peers had taken. I knew I wanted to be able to travel and experience the world the way it was meant to be seen and I've done just that. I've travelled to most places around the world and I'm enjoying every minute of it for sure. In my free time I love to play tennis and believe it or not, compose songs. I wish you all the best again in your endeavours, and may your dreams, whatever they may be, come true abundantly in the near future.

CPSIA information can be obtained
at www.ICGtesting.com
Printed in the USA
LVHW050711241220
675014LV00032B/1340